MILLION DOLLAR MINDSET PRESENTS

POWER

EMOTIONAL INTELLIGENCE

by LINKED IN AND TOWN HALL ACHIEVER OF THE YEAR

EY NOMINEE ENTREPRENEUR OF THE YEAR

GRAND HOMAGE LYS DIVERSITY

Dr. BAK NGUYEN, DMD

TO ALL OF THOSE WISHING FOR MAGIC POWER, YOU HAVE
THEM IN YOU. UNDERSTAND AND MASTER
THEM TO FREE YOUR TRUE SELF.

by Dr. BAK NGUYEN

ISBN: 978-1-989536-08-7

MILLION DOLLAR MINDSET PRESENTS

POWER

EMOTIONAL INTELLIGENCE
by Dr. BAK NGUYEN

INTRODUCTION
BY Dr. BAK NGUYEN

CONCLUSION
BY Dr. BAK NGUYEN

INTRODUCTION

"HARVESTING RAW POWER"

by Dr. BAK NGUYEN

Three days ago, I finished writing my 42nd book, **HOW TO WRITE A BOOK IN 30 DAYS**. It was supposed to be finished today, but I had some spared time, and I pushed the note a little bit…

I wrote and got the book published in 6 days! I was teaching people to do it in 30! So now, you know that it is possible, all you need to do is to start and to keep your **consistency**, following a plan, a template.

Why do I keep pushing so far, so hard? I don't know, maybe because I am trying to feel something! I always told you to go looking for your next win. Mine has to be bigger and bigger so I can feel them.

Yes, I am addicted to my **Momentum** and **success**. To me, there is nothing but win or loss by now. Everything in between is on the loss category.

Do I win all the time? Unfortunately not. I have to learn from my mistake and to keep pushing. Since I found my **Momentum**, I feel less and less; I do not think the difference between a win and a loss anymore… they all blurred as the spin keep accelerating.

I now feel the power, the possibilities, but not always happy. In between, I got a shitty father's day and went crashing down.

Was I exhausted, or was I emptied? I was looking to replenish myself and to have a new book online within the hour wasn't enough anymore to keep my morale up.

This morning, I got two other titles online: **THE STORY OF THE CHICKEN SHIT** and the **BOOK OF LEGENDS 2**. It did help a little to stabilize my mood. But nothing is as powerful as writing a chapter, in a new book!

"I was diving into my emotions. My Momentum kept me afloat."
Dr. Bak Nguyen

If it weren't for my **Momentum**, I would surely have drowned emotionally. **Momentum** is both a ride and a structure giving me stability as I am rising.

"Momentum is the counterweight to my emotional balance."
Dr. Bak Nguyen

The new books franchise, **MILLION DOLLAR MINDSET**, really helped to boost the production of my books. I now have fewer questions to answer as I finish a book, but to know when I'll be starting the next one.

The answer by default to that question is right now!

I was hesitating between writing about **EMOTIONAL INTELLIGENCE** or **BRANDING**. I have much to share on both subjects. It won't be a big miss since, by next week, I am sure that I will be starting the one I didn't pick today.

Intelligence wise, I need to pick the one that inspires me the most so I could surf on my **Momentum**!

"That's EMOTIONAL INTELLIGENCE,
to learn to surf!"
Dr. Bak Nguyen

With my emotions, I've learned to build and to ride **MOMENTUMS**. For those of you who are interested, I covered the subject in my 8th book, **MOMENTUM TRANSFER**, written with coach Dino Masson.

With my emotions, I also got burned more than once. Playing with emotions is like playing with fire, it is appealing from afar, but as you get closer and closer, the heat might meld you down.

In my 15th book, **FORCES OF NATURE**, I described emotions as our ride, our power animal. It was one of the biggest revelations that I uncovered since I started writing.

On one side, we are a big bag of chemical reactions, obeying to the law of nature and our **DNA**. Those are coming from down below; we refer to them as instincts and sensations.

On the other side, we are that sensitivity that records and interprets Life as we come in touch with it. The tastes, the colors, the beauty, the softness, and the odors, they are all within reach, only if we are open to feel and to try.

And yet, we are governing our entire life through our eyes and logic alone. Soon, we've learned to detach from our emotions and to keep them in a cage, locked deep down.

Emotions are dangerous since they will take much power and wisdom to tame. But once you have mastered your feelings, you are unstoppable!

By now, you know that I've embraced the **POWER OF YES**, of openness. That's how my ambition and success went from hustling to thriving. At 42, I am changing the world more than once.

From **Mdex & Co**, I am building a new model for dentistry, the whole industry, changing the way dentistry is delivered and consumed.

My primary clientele is the dentists, but by changing their lives and experience, my work will have an impact on the rest of the world. That's what I call changing the world for the better. That was number 1.

Then, I started writing books. I started and never stopped for the last two years. Today, I have 42 books completed; this is my 43rd within 21 months. Have I changed the world for the better? I surely hope so.

My books might not impact a particular industry, but over time, as the news are spreading, by giving hope and some recipe, I'll be changing the world, life at a time.

But then, I had to package my books and start to record my audiobook. I went through the whole process and wasn't much thrilled about the outcome, and the standards of that industry.

I am not criticizing, just making an observation that much of the world do not read anymore. Those who do, many have turned to the new medium, to learn from an audiobook. I am educating myself with those.

But yet, 65% of the population are visual people, and couldn't only stay concentrate throughout the reading of an audiobook.

With the **EAX, Enhanced Audio Experience**, I brought a new way to read books, appealing to both visual and auditive people.

With the creation of **EAX**, I am changing the world for a second time for the last two years. How did I manage to accomplish all of this? You will find the answer in the **POWER OF YES**, my 36th book.

Even if I told you my story in the **POWER OF YES**, I felt that something was still missing.

I never told you how I managed to transform the raw beauty of nature into energy. This will be the subject of this journey: to open up and to energize.

"The power is both from the outside and from within. To become powerful, one must synchronize both."
Dr. Bak Nguyen

That's what I meant when I said that my success is possible since the day I aligned my emotions and my ambitions. I know that this is a book from **MILLION DOLLAR MINDSET PRESENTS,** so a how-to book.

If I keep the **HOWTO** in the title, it should appear as **HOW TO WIN USING YOUR EMOTIONAL INTELLIGENCE**. I made the cover, but it didn't make the desired impact.

In other words, I didn't feel that it was the right title. **POWER, EMOTIONAL INTELLIGENCE** got me the chills as I was holding the cover in my palm, thought the retina display of my iPhone X. That's the one!

Without hesitating, I scrapped the first cover and went with **POWER**. Some will call it intuition, some, the 6th sense, some, a matter of taste. To me, this is **EMOTIONAL INTELLIGENCE**.

What I felt vibrating in my hand should appealing to other people too. My publishers and marketing team will tell me to keep a consistency in my brand and my titles... Sure, I like branding, but above all, I need to feel.

"What I feel often tells me what to do."
Dr. Bak Nguyen

I succeeded in building more within the last two years than in my entire life combined. What happened? I was open, and I found the power of Momentum. Those two, I covered in **THE POWER OF YES** and **MOMENTUM TRANSFER**. But underneath, there is another secret.

I succeeded because I boosted my **EMOTIONAL INTELLIGENCE**. What is emotional intelligence, and how do we harvest its power? Where and when do we find emotional intelligence? And most importantly, why should we master emotional intelligence?

Just like the last **MILLION DOLLAR MINDSET**'s book, **WHAT, WHEN, WHERE, WHY**, and **HOW** will be at the center of this book.

May you find your answer within the next pages and chapter to guide you through your journey. I know that by writing those lines, I am already feeling better.

"To grow, one must share."
Dr. Bak Nguyen

This is both a gift and a burden, but since I feel good doing it, it became my call and my passion: to empower you through your journey to find yourself.

EMOTIONAL INTELLIGENCE is the third ingredient to success and to keep winning. The other two were **MOMENTUM** and **OPENNESS**. Combine the three, and you will be surfing the flow of Evolution, the flow of Life.

Welcome to **MILLION DOLLAR MINDSET**. This is **POWER, EMOTIONAL INTELLIGENCE**.

This book is not about understanding EMOTIONAL INTELLIGENCE, but about accessing its POWER.

Dr. BAK NGUYEN

CHAPTER 1

"TO START GATHERING INTELLIGENCE"

by Dr. BAK NGUYEN

From childhood, we've been trained to think with our head. What we see, what we touch is what we believe exists. Slowly, we've been led to believe that whatever we don't see or don't understand does not exist. What a flaw!

It will not be easy to reboot our beliefs system, but trust me, it is possible. Have you ever played poker? How do you win? By looking at your cards or by reading the other players? Will they tell you what they hold in they hand? And if they do, can you believe them?

Pretty simple as an example to understand that there is more than meet the eyes!

The **CIA** trains their agent to read body languages and to detect a change in pulse and to breathe to understand how someone is lying and deforming the truth.

We all saw those karate and kong fu master who lost their sight, only to become even more powerful, because they now see with their whole body, not only their eyes. They have many words to describe the phenomena, but merging with the universe is one of the common them. Neo, in the **MATRIX**, combines with the system.

They are from a different time, different culture, and yet, they all come to the same conclusion, tapping in the same source of energy.

Don't worry; you won't have to lose your sight to understand the power within this book, you only have to expand your scope and your comprehension beyond what you already know.

"To feel is our most basic skills.
We were born with that skill."
Dr. Bak Nguyen

Even as a baby, we could feel. With the year, some will keep that ability, and some will forget about it. Fear, sadness, joy, love, those are the feelings that we retained. What about the others?

To have the feeling that someone is watching you, to have the impression that something is not right, to smell that danger is coming.

No, you are not a heretic nor a weirdo; you tapped into your body and felt the world around you.

"Feeling is information, nothing more
and nothing less."
Dr. Bak Nguyen

The sad thing is that in our culture and society, we have invented many words to mask our ignorance. We ridicule those who feel, labeling them as crazies, chickens, and witches. In our perception, we have evolved since we burned those people. Today we treat them with medication and drugs.

The reality is that we are just scared of what we don't comprehend. We are also too proud to accept that beyond our understanding, lays a whole world, the universe.

What is not accessible to our intelligence, we discard. Then, we fill the void lies and folklore. This is our legacy. No worries, we won't be talking about magic, witches or any dark powers. I don't have that kind of knowledge.

On the other hand, a little history lesson helps to put into perspective what we missed all those years. **EMOTIONAL INTELLIGENCE** is natural and more intuitive than our logic and everything we learned from school and society.

To read people, to feel what is coming, tapping in the energy of the universe, those are all facets of the **EMOTIONAL INTELLIGENCE**.

Let's start to cover our legacy, the one we received from the universe and God, shall we?

"Emotional Intelligence is a gift from God.
Why waste it?"
Dr. Bak Nguyen

To define what is **EMOTIONAL INTELLIGENCE** will be a mistake, to begin with. We are trying to leave our head aside for a moment, not double down on it. Do we feel love, or do we understand love?

Step one of **EMOTIONAL INTELLIGENCE**, information gathering.

It is always easier to look that the others than to look at ourselves since we see ourselves through many, many filters and presets – the first to understand the feeling of others.

By the way, do you know why the **CIA** is studying the body language? Because the body can hardly lie. The tongue is pretty agile and have been trained to manipulate the truth, but not the body.

On the same line of thought, how many people can lie about how they feel? They can choose to ignore it, and they often do because they do not know how to react with such feelings.

To keep the appearance of control, they discard their feelings.

Since they discarded their feeling out of fear of losing control, do you think that they have a clue of how to lie with and from the emotions? Not a chance. To gather that information in to gather raw data about the other party.

Do you have a better idea of the power within this book yet?

> "The first rule of emotional intelligence is sympathy."
> Dr. Bak Nguyen

SYMPATHY

There is more than one way to start; this is the easiest and the one I know the best. The best way to approach someone is to make them feel at ease with you.

Be sympathetic and have them open up. You'll be surprised how much you can learn from smiling and staying silent.

Do that often, do that with consistency and soon enough, you will be the guest that people are looking to surround themselves with.

"Being a good listener is the easiest way to start to gather intelligence. But nothing is free in life…"
Dr. Bak Nguyen

Soon enough, you will find yourself with a mountain of data to sort from. I said it was smooth, not painless! But I wanted you to try that first since conventional wisdom will tell you to listen more than you talk.

The key was the listening you were applying. You can listen passively and have mountains of data to sort from, or you can listen actively and sort of the source the information you are gathering.

ACTIVE LISTENING

Once again, there are many definitions of **ACTIVE LISTENING**; let me give you mine. Start by talking, take the lead. Keep being sympathetic and convivial but talk until you have established the perimeter of the discussion.

To set a **perimeter** is not something for a novice, but with practice, this will prove to be a good use for you if you do not want to spend hours and hours sorting through mountains of data!

"Everybody lies."
Dr. Gregory House

I learned that from the tremendous medical show, **EVERYBODY LIES**. Keep that in mind. When you are passively listening, how do you sort out the lies from the truth? That will prove to be a challenge.

But if you are listening actively, you have set the **dialogue's perimeter**.

In other words, you know the field and can have the advantage of the discussion since you know all the reference of your perimeter and will know soon enough when someone is bullshitting you.

And again, do not stop at the first layer. That someone lies is a piece of information, but imperfect information. The metadata is way more relevant here! Now that you know that they lie to try to understand why they lied?

Everything you might uncover from here is valuable information that might serve you in the future. It won't be as hard as you think, that since you know they were lying, you do not have to listen to them anymore, all you have to do is to read them.

You are in gathering mode, and the sorting and labeling happened on the spot, not painfully after the facts.

Do you want an example to wrap your mind around the concept?

I am a dentist, let use that example to illustrate the concept. A patient that I never met presents himself at a consultation. The first question after the greetings is: **HOW CAN I HELP YOU**?

I will give him total attention for the next 5 minutes as he is telling me his needs and desires. Then, I will address his problem talking about what I see as a problem and how we will address the issue.

Dentistry is a technical science, and yet, I won't be spending much time talking about the technics nor the skills involved. I will be spending time on how he'll feel throughout the process, how fast the surgery will be, and how long it will take him to heal.

In other words, he started a story which I gave a body and a development. Now stop talking and look at him. Something the silence will be awkward.

If he is asking me how much it will cost, I know that he is severe and will be looking forward to receiving treatment. If he is asking questions about the procedure, I know that he is interested.

Now, if he spends too much time talking about the procedure, he is telling you that he is insecure. He is still fishing at this stage.

If he spends much time about the cost, you know that he is dangerous, but too much time will also be telling you that he is still shopping around.

They are nothing wrong about shopping around. The information you should have from this is that you did not make much of an impression, you are a mere commodity, that why he is comparing you on the matter of money. This is not an absolute, but it will give you much to think on.

If what he is asking is when can we start or how soon he will have to make the payments, you know that you hit a core. This answer he is telling you is that you have his trust, and he feels secure within your hands.

As a cosmetic dentist, that's the game. This can be applied to any other field as long as there is a matter of discussion and negotiation involved.

As a dentist, I do not intend to read and to analyze everyone in front of me. My goal is to better myself and to perfect my craft, making a diagnostic and communication the plan of treatment to my patient.

If they feel safe, I know that I was efficient and appreciate. If they are getting out of that appointment with hope, I have done my duty, at least the first part!

On the other hand, I leverage on every single one of those visits to evaluate how far I have pushed my craft, making people at ease.

How long consultation took, what kind of questions were involved, and of course, the outcome, those are all data that I sort and analyze to keep improving on my performance.

I went from giving people 1 hour of consultation went I first started to around 10-15 minutes today. Don't get me wrong, I am never in a rush, and I will take all the time I needed to do my consultation.

The worst thing that you want your patient to keep from that consultation is that you are in a rush and they aren't necessary!

"Reading people is a two-way street."
Dr. Bak Nguyen

Your goal here is to leave the information that you want, while you gather the information you need. In this example, to give them support and establish trust on the one hand, and to understand what are they looking for on the other.

All of this at the dentist within 15 minutes, will you have ever imagined that you are giving that much away?

SYMPATHY through **Active listening** is the first key to **EMOTIONAL INTELLIGENCE**.

Welcome to **MILLION DOLLAR MINDSET**. This is **POWER, EMOTIONAL INTELLIGENCE**.

EMOTIONAL INTELLIGENCE POWER

Dr. BAK NGUYEN

CHAPTER 2

"TO PREDICT THE FUTURE"

by Dr. BAK NGUYEN

In the last chapter, we learned how to listen... efficiently. I want to clarify, this is not the only way to look and to gather information, but if you are healthy and confident enough to take the lead with leaking important information, you have the advantage.

There is still the matter of confidence here. We will come back on that subject later on. For now, there is much more ground to cover.

Remember that everyone lies and how that was only the first layer of information? If you have established that the subject is lying, the metadata coming with it will prove of great resource: why did that person lie? To what end?

All much more exciting and important questions to focus on if you are thinking of doing business or to have a relationship with that person. Oh, get over it, everyone lies, and so are you, so don't be misled, but don't play the rapped victims either!

"Know you who are talking to, know yourself, and then, only then, deal."
Dr. Bak Nguyen

What is the next phase of **EMOTIONAL INTELLIGENCE**? To be able to do something useful with the intelligence gathered.

Just like the poker player is reading people to defeat them and call out their bluff, the CIA agent is looking to plot or to find out the other side's plot; you should have a clear goal in mind.

"In the game of society, make up your mind,
are you playing defense or offense.
There is not much in between."
Dr. Bak Nguyen

You cannot gather intelligence for the sake of gathering information. In that case, you are often wasting your resources and time.

Worst you are giving away valuable intelligence about yourself, and whatever you've gathered may not be as relevant in the future.

"Like anything else, gathered intelligence
has an expiration date."
Dr. Bak Nguyen

EMPATHY

So what is the next phase of **EMOTIONAL INTELLIGENCE**? Now that you know what you are standing for and what you are playing for, you still have to learn with whom you are playing with.

Unfortunately, the listen actively is far from enough to understand you who are facing.

"Ally or foe, you still need to understand
the person in front of you better."
Dr. Bak Nguyen

The best way to do so is to be that person. Is that even possible? The closest way I know what to be a person, in other words, to understand how it feels like to walk in his/her shoes, is called **EMPATHY**.

In our society, **EMPATHY** is used to qualify a good human being caring for others. He/she is kind and sensitive, always ready to help and to listen.

That's true, but not accurate nor complete. The description you just read is the description of what people felt in the presence of an empathetic person.

Now, that empathetic person is way more complicated than just making the other party feel at ease.

Because they were at ease, they open up, and they share. If you know what you are looking for, you can either dig and sort the mountain of information they are spitting out. Or you are analyzing the mind frame and the mindset of your counterpart.

Doing so, try to understand what he is looking for, why is he here? What motivates him/her, and what scars him/her? From a lie that you can confirm, you have now correct metadata to work upon.

If you keep poking that person, he/she will be too busy covering up his/her lies to understand what you are doing, reading his/her play. Doing so, you can have a good idea of his/her mindset and frame of mind.

It is not accurate, but you can then ask some question and see how he/she will react.

"No matter the answer, look for the HOW
and the WHY, not the WHAT."
Dr. Bak Nguyen

41

Now that you have successfully uncovered part of his/her mindset, motivation and goal, you can project yourself in their shoes to understand how he/she will be reacting to a stimulus, any stimulus.

This is when you provoke situations and opportunities to see how that person will be reacting.

Doing so, whatever his/her reaction, you had a template in your mind, so you can pinpoint what was right and what was wrong quickly and with precision unless that person knows what you are up to and is deliberately playing you.

If that's the case, this is a master game! You might be in over your head. Take your loss and walk out.

On the contrary, if you feel aroused by the challenge, you just found a worthy opponent. On the field, you might be playing the opposite side, but just like a dance, if you both have the respect of each other, you've only found a dance partner.

Go with what your body is telling you, go with what your **EMOTIONAL INTELLIGENCE** is stirring you toward.

"It's hard enough to win and to be ahead.
Don't fight yourself on top of that!"
Dr. Bak Nguyen

That's what I meant by listening to your inner feeling. Do what you feel like doing, even if it is unsecured and new, you are having the opportunity of a lifetime.

On the other hand, if you are forcing yourself from social pressure, orders, hierarchy to do something you don't feel right, you are losing **3/4 of your potential** already!

Three quarter? Yes, since your emotional intelligence is not with you but against you, you are playing at **half your power**.

Then, whatever half is left, half of that will be to convince you that you have enough confidence and strength to face the challenge.

A simple example of that is in our childhood. Why is it that some students just scored trophy after trophy? It's because they love to win, and since they have tasked victory, their emotions and their ambitions aligned. They are just eager to go back on the field to bite in their next win!

The other player is grinding and hoping. Most of the time, he/she will fell in the trap of jealousy and start blaming everyone else but themselves. That's one option.

There are also those who looked up to the champion and said that they would never be as good. They are discouraging themselves and feel both heavy and guilty. They are kicking their behind to just show up at the training.

Either way, the two last contenders is far behind to ever compete with the champion. If the hero was at full potential, even a little more since he/she is motivated, the other two are playing with less than half their potential, sometimes even with just a quarter.

What are the odds of 110% versus 50% or even 25%? And as the streak of wins continues, the difference of the odds will be more significant and greater.

That's **EMOTIONAL INTELLIGENCE**. Even if there did know about it, not apply its principles willingly, the same outcome would come out of the play.

"This book is not about understanding EMOTIONAL INTELLIGENCE, but about accessing its POWER."

Dr. Bak Nguyen

I read a few days ago on the social media an interesting quote:

$$0.99^{30} \text{ is } 0.73 \text{ while } 1.01^{30} \text{ is } 1.36.$$

What this means in everyday's language is that even if you are giving it your 99% and you keep doing it day after day for a month, you end up about half of the result of the other who score 101%. 2% more compounded over a month. Can you imagine the math on 365 days?

I was surprised myself of the simple logic of numbers behind the equation. Why is it that 99% will bring you

46

to fail as miserably? Because you are spending time and energy and are not receiving any back in return. You are mainly depleting yourself more and more.

The reactivity is even worst. Think of :

$$0.50^{30} \text{ is } 0.000\ 000\ 000\ 465\ 661$$

This is why and how Life looked so unfair to many. They got their math wrong.

To remedy the situation, go in with you 100% and give it all what you got to top it at 101%. That's a win! Build from that win and keep building.

"It's not enough to never give up. One still needs to be complete to have a chance to win."
Dr. Bak Nguyen

That's what I meant when I said to align your **EMOTIONS** and your **AMBITIONS**. Do so, and you are whole, at 100%, ready to race. Keep doing so, and each time you be growing, not depleting.

Do that with the knowledge of **EMPATHY** and what are the odds now? You are coming in full speed, and you can predict how the other player will react. Get your 101%!

For those who are facing a superior mind, playing the same game that you are playing, if you were at 100% and you still lose that game, that's mean that the other was at 101%!

In other words, the other party outsmarted you! That should give you the motivation to come back, even more, fire up to win back what you thought was yours!

This is one of the best case scenarios since both of you will be enrolling in a competition forcing the other always to top their own game. This is the closest to a friendship you might have.

Isn't the game getting interesting? Improve your odds and start winning. It is ok to be addicted to something, especially winning!

With **EMPATHY**, you have a tool to predict the future, at least, the one of your counterpart. Showing up at 100%, you have an excellent chance to win. Aim for that 101%!

We started this chapter talking about predicting the future. You are already writing the future. But this is the subject of the next section.

EMPATHY is the second key to **EMOTIONAL INTELLIGENCE**.

Welcome to **MILLION DOLLAR MINDSET**. This is **POWER, EMOTIONAL INTELLIGENCE**.

EMOTIONAL INTELLIGENCE **POWER**

Dr. BAK NGUYEN

CHAPTER 3

"TO BE IN HARMONY"

by Dr. BAK NGUYEN

It is getting more and more enjoyable. Now that you have the power to predict how the other party will react? How do you feel?

You read right, how do you feel? This is one of the most important questions one must ask oneself regularly.

If you know how you feel, it's the beginning of the **day**, your day. If you accept how you feel, it's the beginning of your **path**. And if you react to how you think, it's the beginning of your **rise**.

It sounds like poetry, but it is the best thing one can do for oneself. You can be selfless, but still, need to be aware. You can be generous, but again, need to replenish. You can be kind and always be receptive to your needs.

INFLUENCE

Now that you know how the other will react, would it be cool to stir him/her in a right direction? **INFLUENCE** is the third key to **EMOTIONAL INTELLIGENCE**.

Some people will be talking of **MANIPULATION**, others, of **INFLUENCE**. It is mainly the same since each person has the power to make up their mind and to make their choice.

If we need a distinction between **MANIPULATION** and **INFLUENCE**, it is in the **HOW**. As a person is manipulated, often, he/she wasn't fed all of the information to be able to make his/her decision. In the worst case scenario, they've been fed lies. Yes, it is despicable and dishonest.

In the case of **INFLUENCE**, it is a different story. The person is being educated and well informed on the alternatives at hand and the foreseeable outcomes. Nothing is 100%, but in science and medicine, we call it to make an educated guess.

To influence someone is to help that person to see the consequences of their actions and the outcome of a course of operations, even the result of **NO ACTION**.

To be influent, you must be credible and trustworthy first. Then you must be knowledgable and to have a clear and robust vision of the whereabouts and the final destination.

"It's not about you; it's about them."
Dr. Bak Nguyen

The rule of **INFLUENCE** makes it about them, always. That's how you will keep people's attention. As you understand their needs and their pain with **EMPATHY**, you can now help them to see clearly and to take specific **ACTIONS** to remedy the situation.

Often, your **INFLUENCE** grows from the fact that you are helping them. The more that you are useful to them and that their pain finds a solution within your words, you will grow and spread your **INFLUENCE**. That's a form of **POWER**.

Are you ready to learn about the power of **INFLUENCE**?

The first rule is to know and understand your audience. Through **ACTIVE LISTENING**, **SYMPATHY**, and

EMPATHY, you now have the means to understand the other party and to feel what they feel.

That, can you guess what they want? Not always, why not ask them? Yes, as a doctor, that's the first question that I ask my patient, what can I do for you?

Usually, people are open to answer honestly that question, not all the time, but most of the time. If you have that as a reference, you can now base your line of action from where they are right now to where they want to be.

EMPATHY well indicated to you how they would react at each step of the way. We all want more than what we have, why is it that so few are moving forward?

Because even if they know what they want, they cannot see past the next step to take, and that step, they are not willing to do! Until the pain becomes real...

Tell them in advance what is laying ahead, right ahead. As they will see it, they will remember your words. The first time, they will think that you were lucky, but by the second and third time, they will take you seriously. The only question is, will you still be around?

"Influence is to tell someone what will be
and to have no expectation."
Dr. Bak Nguyen

Most of us hate to be sold. We do not like salespeople in general. The best way to avoid that label as a leader is to not depend on the outcome from your words.

If they feel that they had much to gain from the wisdom and advice, they might consider it. Of course, everything is bilateral in Life!

"To last, everything must be a two-way street."
Dr. Bak Nguyen

So yes, you might be gaining something out of it. Be upfront with it; be transparent. Doing so, we will not be labeled with **MANIPULATION**. That word helps such a negative connotation.

Again, those people asking from you everything and refusing that you will have nothing out of it were not your audience. Read in between the lines: they are haters and none believers only out to poke holes in your vibe. Ignore them.

Unfortunately, those haters will be the loudest. Some from jealousy, some from ignorance, some just because that's the way they are. Expect that to happen as soon as you start to matter, that you gain a level of influence.

Know your audience. Feel their pain and tell them what will come next. Not in ten years, tomorrow. Give them something small that they can experience. Then, give them the fix.

Start small and keep doing it day after day. By the third time, you will have gained their trust. Your **INFLUENCE** is growing. On one-on-one, start with something small, start something within reach and grow your influence from there.

On the matter, here's a real-life example:

My son of 8 years old, William Bak is writing books with me for the last six months. Together we have 19 books to this date. I started writing with William because he asked me to write a book with him.

From one, we finished at three within a matter of weeks:

- THE LEGEND OF THE CHICKEN HEART
- THE LEGEND OF THE LION HEART
- THE LEGEND OF THE DRAGON HEART

Then, I learned that he is failing his French class at 55%. We were about to set new world record writing together, to deal with the failure of his French class was a significant drag.

"Align your emotions and your ambitions, and you are unstoppable. Harmony is compelling."
Dr. Bak Nguyen

So to have him improve his French's skills, I made him translate all his book from English to French, sentence by sentence. Of course, I was proof-writing along the way.

I gave him pride writing book, I motivate him to translate in French, and within three months, he went from 55% to 80%! That's a vast improvement.

In the meantime, he kept pushing me to write more and more books with him. I got him invested in his success and had him commit to doing more and more.

Today, the worst thing that I can say to him is to fire him from our partnership writing books! He found his destiny, according to his own words!

He keeps trying to please me and to make sure that I stay by his side to write more books. I didn't put any pressure on him; he put the pressure on me.

As he was getting happier and happier about his books piling up on the Apple store, he had something to protect: his legacy (again, his own words).

He started writing because he saw me doing so. He wanted the same. Then, he got involved and shared the joy of performing. He later learned the fear of losing what he got.

Since we started writing together, I do not have to reprimand him much; he makes sure that I am happy and keep him on board. That's **Influence** times two! (Copying and then, pleasing).

Mainly I got him to act in ways that I wish for. Am I controlling? Sure, but not in ways that he can revolt from. I got his feelings and ambitions (even at eight years old) aligned, and he followed the logic.

I said to start small. This is not small to me; it is enormous! I have upgraded that's my role as a father. Today, William is a buddy, my best buddy! We share a relationship and a connection beyond father and son. We are connected.

I opened up, and I listen. I understood and aligned his emotions and his ambitions. Then, I supported both his progress and his feelings, and I let his fears and agreed to guide him through his journey, the beginning of his life.

Simple steps, adding up, compiling. The keys of **EMOTIONAL INTELLIGENCE** will help you throughout your entire life. The sooner you master the skills, the more you can leverage on them and enjoy!

Active listening, **Empathy**, **Influence** are all keys to **EMOTIONAL INTELLIGENCE**. I believe that **HARMONY** is just that, to align your emotions and your ambitions. Doing so, you are whole!

Find your **HARMONY** first and then; you might gain the **Power of Influence**. Feel the power and the potential you hold. You now have the Power, to predict not only the future, but also the Power to write the future!

Welcome to **MILLION DOLLAR MINDSET**. This is **POWER, EMOTIONAL INTELLIGENCE**.

CHAPTER 4

"TO BUILD A PATHWAY TO THE FUTURE"

by Dr. BAK NGUYEN

Now that you have harvested the power of Influence, would you mind amplifying it? After having felt, understood, and influenced the thought process of one person, how about doing it on a significant number of people, a crowd?

To influence a crowd is a whole another game than to change a single person. It will take many keys of **EMOTIONAL INTELLIGENCE** to touch and move many people all at once.

In a crowd, some will believe in one thing, while others will find in the exact opposite. How do you manage to keep the core of the group moving your way?

"The first rule of influence, be confident!"
Dr. Bak Nguyen

Owe your word, own the space, owe the attention. To do so, you must be both **HONEST** and **BOLD**, **VULNERABLE**, and **CONFIDENT**.

By being **HONEST**,

You **OPEN** communication.

By being **BOLD**,

You have a chance to **APPEAL** to people.

By being **VULNERABLE**,

You give people a chance to **RELATE**.

By being **CONFIDENT**,

You give people **HOPE**.

"The pain has to be greater than the pain of change
for you to gain INFLUENCE with the least resistance. "
Dr. Bak Nguyen

The pain of change, that's a concept that I covered in my first book, **SYMPHONY OF SKILLS**. The idea is that most people don't like to change!

Laziness, fear, complacency are all factors that add up to the equation. Our society has evolved more as settlers than travelers and nomads, that's why we do not like change, any change.

Throughout the centuries, this characteristic has come to become dominant in most of our **DNA** and mindset.

The only strong emotions that will make people accept change quickly are fear and pain. Even if some people freeze as they are scared, most will find the will and strength to react and to get out of the danger zone.

This has been an old trick exploited in politic to have crowds to move in a specific direction. If the fear is real, that's **INFLUENCE**. If the concern is manufactured, that's **MANIPULATION**.

Unfortunately, the line has been blurred more and more between those two. Today, with all of the information available and at our fingertips, it has come more to a matter of **INTENT** to differentiate between **INFLUENCE** and **MANIPULATION**.

"Help people, and you are on the right path of INFLUENCE. Don't argue, look into your heart."
Dr. Bak Nguyen

This book is about showing you to master power, the power of **EMOTIONAL INTELLIGENCE**. You will be free to use that power to what you deem worthy. Please know that it will also come at a price, the consequences of your words and your actions.

Now that you are more and more skillful, with **EMOTIONAL INTELLIGENCE**, the weight of your words is well over the scope of an average person, of a member of the crowd.

You are still a person, but now, you are a leader. Your words and your actions will be well amplified by those who are listening to you, who believe in you.

Through your words, there will take steps. Please be kind and consequential.

"With great powers come great responsibilities."
Stan Lee

I think that you get the picture. I have teased you long enough. Are you ready to learn about the **POWER OF MOMENTUM FROM THE CROWD**?

The first rule is to know and understand your audience. Through **ACTIVE LISTENING**, **SYMPATHY**, and **EMPATHY**, you now have the means to understand the other party and to feel what they feel. With **INFLUENCE**, you are now guiding people to join your line of thoughts.

Know your audience. Feel their pain and tell them what will come next. Not in ten years, tomorrow. Give them something small that they can experience. Then, give them the fix.

Start small and keep doing it day after day. By the third time, you will have gained their trust. Your **INFLUENCE** is now growing. On one-on-one, that's the way to increase your **INFLUENCE**. With a crowd, that's another story, another game!

If you are trying to influence more than two people at a time, you are trying to influence an audience. You will have to up your game.

How can you relate to more than one person at a time? Tell them a story, can that they can refer to. If that is your story, it is even better, since it will be the most credible.

Tell them a story to identify the audience.
Tell them a story to identify the pain.

Tell them a story to help them see the journey.

With the **Power of Narrative** (Storytelling), you have the chance to have people relating to your hero.

In other words, since you do not have the time and the opportunity to know them one by one, have them to identify with you. Some will if your story is compelling.

Then, focus on those who are reading from your lips to **ACTIVELY LISTEN** through the way they are reacting to your words.

EMPATHY is harder on a crowd, but once again, if you are confident enough and your speech is genuine, you will have the opportunity to feel **THE PULSE** of the group, as a collective. That's exhilarating; you should try it!

Of course, in the crowd, some will like you, and some will not. Most of the group will be listening, trying to decide what to make out of your words.

Stay confident, no matter the reaction, and keep telling your story with calm. If the crowd is reacting in your favor, empower it by feeding in a frenzy! Then, make sure to bring them back to your pace, to your tone of voice.

If you can have the crowd beating at your heartbeat, you know that they are with you. Not all of them, but since there is a crowd pressuring effect, half if the group will be feeling a vibe and give in to it.

"The key is to have them feel the right vibe, yours!"
Dr. Bak Nguyen

Whatever you do, if you are doing something, people will react to you. In a group of 10 people, two will love and praise you; three will raise their voices and trash you, five will stay silent. Who can you believe?

Those three trashing you! You see, we have been raised in a society where it usually not cool to voice your opinions. Whatever you said have affected them to the point that they had to speak up! They are the one telling the truth: that what you do change them.

Those two praising you, you will never really know what they are thinking. Do not give to much credit to them. Accept them gradually, but do not base your actions on their reactions.

The real balance resides in those five remaining silence. They are looking at you and are making up their minds. They will even enjoy seeing the haters throwing arrows at you. The way you react will be telling them how to qualify you.

If you want to win their votes, be the bigger man/woman, respond to the arrow in kind and keep pushing your narrative forward. The more **CONFIDENT** you are, even after an attack, the more they will start joining you.

With that, the crowd effect will start to show its impact, and even the haters will be joining in, eventually.

It not **how many** people rally behind you that is important here. It is **how fast** you can gather a **majority of the crowd** behind you. How fast, since a group can easily change its mind as quickly as the wind can change.

"Ride the crowd as you are surfing the waves.
Nothing last forever, nothing is stable.
But it can be fluid, though."
Dr. Bak Nguyen

As Dr. Bak, I had the many opportunities to speak in from of hundreds of people at once. Every time, I am delivering a message of hope, that it is possible for everyone.

Every single time, I gain my inspiration and my **Momentum** looking at one or two people in the crowd, reacting well to my words and ideas. I sometimes even address them directly.

That's a good tip for a public speaker, relate to your crowd, literally. Those who are skeptical, if they have raised their concerns, I even develop a dialogue with them, from the stage.

Very often, they will have concerns, but won't be pressured more than one a two points, since they do not have the answer either.

I respond to them respectfully, addressing their request and giving them **HOPE**. I try not to give them much attention since I do not want them to **pace** my speech. I am only answering to them so the crowd can know that I am not hiding.

"Act respectfully and gracefully;
those are my secrets."
Dr. Bak Nguyen

Even when I did not have the answer, this line of conduct has always stood by me and done me great good.

To insert some humor is a great way to break the tension and to connect with your audience. I remember how I started my speaking career, introducing myself as such:

"Hi, I am Dr. Bak. I am a dentist. (Pause) Every time that I said that I'd lost half my friends already… "

Every time, I succeed to have people laugh. That put them at ease to start a conversation with me. Yes, a conversation. Just like I said that writing a book is a dialogue, to deliver a speech in public is also a dialogue, a dance between you and your audience.

"Respect them, love them,
and make them love you!"
Dr. Bak Nguyen

Dance your way throw the crowd, change partner, make them dream, move them, listen to them, but always, keep the lead.

Pacing your speech and your tone is also of prime importance. What is the right pace? The one that you felt from the feedback of your public. What tone should you adopt? The one that you feel comfortable having.

By now, you know how to leverage your **EMOTIONAL INTELLIGENCE**; you know how to feel the crowd. Whatever is making you comfortable is what will appeal to your audience… if not, you won't be feeling that comfortable.

"Confidence is sexy."
Dr. Bak Nguyen

This is one of my famous and favorite quotes. But, on stage, there is nothing more authentic and real! Be confident, be bold, be honest. That's how people will follow you as you speak and will respect your leadership.

Because yes, the only way to gain influence is to assume the position of a leader. Power is a skill that needs much mastering and craft. It will take the mastering of your power of both your **Sympathy** and **Empathy**.

On top of that, it will require you to be **honest** and **confident** at the same time. You need to be **open** and **vulnerable** enough for people to **relate** to you and, at the same time, be sure **confident** for people to follow you.

There is no secret recipe here other than to practice and practice skill by skill until it becomes second nature.

To gain Momentum from the **force of the crowd**, that is the power of this chapter. Much more technical than the previous section, it can prove to be among the most powerful.

POWER coming from **EMOTIONS**, that the key to **Momentum**. The crowd will not understand a word of what you are saying. They will feel your heart, and they will synchronize their heartbeat to yours.

That's the harmony that you are looking for, that the **CROWD EMPOWERMENT** that will get you both **speed** and **altitude**.

To speak to a crowd is not something that is given to everyone. But it is a skill required to be a leader of men, of women, a person with the power of changing the world through his/her words and thoughts alone.

You didn't need to be smart to gain such power; you required to synchronize the crowd to your heartbeat and the tone of your voice.

Through **Active listening**, **Empathy**, **Influence**, and now **Momentum of the Crowd**, you now hold 5 of the key of **EMOTIONAL INTELLIGENCE**.

Feel the power and the potential you hold. You are getting closer and closer to the mastering of your inner strength! No future can be built by one person alone.

The Power of the Crowd will give you the **Momentum** to act in unison, to unite, and to make a difference. Use your power for good, remember that each action has its consequence.

Welcome to **MILLION DOLLAR MINDSET**. This is **POWER, EMOTIONAL INTELLIGENCE**.

This book is not about understanding EMOTIONAL INTELLIGENCE, but about accessing its POWER

Dr. BAK NGUYEN

CHAPTER 5
"TO WRITE THE FUTURE"
by Dr. BAK NGUYEN

How powerful do you feel? I showed you the potential; you still have to build up your core first. And your heart, what is it? Your heart, your single focus is your **Confidence**.

"Confidence is sexy!"
Dr. Bak Nguyen

I know, I said it already and I will repeat it.

Without **Confidence**, this no **genuine**.

Without **Confidence**, there is no **boldness**.

Without **Confidence**, there is no **charm**

Nor **presence**.

Is **Confidence** everything? As a leader, a builder, a dreamer, you bet! **Emotional Intelligence** is about leveraging upon who and what you are to move forward. How can you move forward denying who you are, deep down?

I showed you the potential and the **power of Emotional Intelligence** way beyond the scope of technics and secrets. I showed you the road and the means. That's the body, that's part 2.

You will still need to figure out what is your end goal, your destination. That's part 3. But before you begin, part 1 is to know who you are, to built and leverage from it. That part is called **Confidence**.

I cannot tell you how to build your **Confidence**. I can only tell you how I made mine and my son's.

You see, I am a multiple genii. I can create as fast as I breathe. I am both sensitive and artistic. On the other hand, I have a logic that is hard to beat, and when I am executing, I am hot as fire and intense focus on the task at hand. Don't stand in my way!

Because society and my parent wanted something else out of me, I had to grow and to adapt. Forty years I am adapting made me into the **perfect hybrid** that I am.

A few years ago, a mentor of mine, Dr. Mohamed Benkhalifa, asked me to take the Gallup test of Intelligence. That test is measuring the kind of intelligence one has. There are 30 types of Intelligence, according to the Gallup Institute.

Usually, a person will score between 4-5 types of Intelligence. The most gifted people will score up to 8 types of Intelligence.

For this book, I will share with you my result: I scored 22 types of Intelligence. No, I am not bragging, but not at all.

I was so in disbelief that I retook the test 3 times to make sure that it was accurate. Every time, I scored between 20 and 22 types of Intelligence!

Growing up, I could never stand in place for a long time. Back then, we were not diagnosed with anything. By today's standards, I would inevitably be labeled as **A.D.D** (Attention Deficit Disorder).

Thank God, I was not medicated and just had to do my part to fit in.

At school, I was often in trouble because I was either defying the teacher on his/her teaching or just merely disinterested. To my parents, I was such a burden. I am the elders of a family of three, and they had the hands full just with me.

Coming from an immigrant family, I was causing trouble where there was no time to spare for such none sense! So I grew up hearing that I was an idiot!

No, I know that I am smart, but compare to my siblings and my cousins, I was a trouble maker. All they had to do is to show up at school, and everyone loved them, especially the teachers.

Me, I always had a harder time fitting in. I was edgy. Then, even if I tried, I could never score that 95 % or 100%. I was more compelled to spend the least amount of time studying and still beat the average. That was my mindset.

I was wasting my talents and the sweat of my parents according to them. I wasn't a good student, but I tried my best to be a good son. So I adapted to the best of my capabilities.

I accepted the fact that I was an idiot. I was okay with it. Don't get me wrong, it was painful, but I developed the ability to heal… leaving some scars behind.

I graduated as a doctor in dentistry, not quickly, but I graduated. Today I am among the loved cosmetic surgeon in dentistry. My patients come from around the world!

I was never the best at school, but that was fine by me. I was always under the expectations of my parents, and I learned to cope with it. I was an idiot compared to the rest of my family. I accepted it.

In truth, it took me years to heal and to accept who I was, one with many Bits of Intelligence. They were calling me arrogant, as I was expressing my views. I was shy then. Today, I am much much bolder, and people are calling that leadership!

What is most surprising is that my mentors all said that I was among the most humble person that they ever trained. Humble? Really? I spent my life being labeled arrogant!

It took me years to forgive myself and to accept who I am. It took even longer for me to respect myself. But as I finally did, I am now whole and thriving!

Within the last 24 months, I've accomplished more than I had in the first 40 years! Of course, I am building on top of what I was, but in entirely different and unrelated fields. From dentistry, I went on to be a visionary businessman.

From Business, I went to become a world record (to be confirmed) author with 43 books written within 21 months. From the author, I am now starting my motivational speaking career!

Trust me, more than my introduction as a dentist to have people laughing, I am learning everything from the ground up!

Many factors are explaining my rise, but the core and key are the following:

"I've finally aligned my emotions and my ambitions. With that, my wings grew back."
Dr. Bak Nguyen

In other words, I am now at peace and confident with myself. About what I know and what I don't. About what I can and what I will. **Confidence** is vital, **Confidence** is sexy.

I learned to listen to myself, my inner voice. I learned to trust my instincts and do not care about opinions. If I am looking for views, it is to understand the market, not to be judged.

I learned, to be humble and honest while respecting myself. I am a man of action and my word. That being said, I am not stupid and will not be manipulated because I said so. It has to make sense.

Today, I am still in the process of discovering my capability and powers. I don't know what is my destiny, but I am embracing each day with **Hope**, with **Confidence**.

About my past, I hold nothing but **Gratitude**. Could it have been easier? Maybe, but it could also be harder.

I received, and I made the most out of what I was given. I am not asking of more.

"What has changed, though, is that now, it is up to me to set the expectations!"
Dr. Bak Nguyen

That's how I've come to grow into Dr. Bak.

Now, about William Bak, my son. From his first year, I've learned much looking at him. As he was feeding as a baby, I was covering the night shift, from 12 AM to 6 AM.

I never saw so many sunrises in my entire life! And that was among the wonders I've discovered as a dad. Holding him in my arms as he was sleeping peacefully, I had much time to love and to reflect: How can I keep that peace that he is born with?

"He is at peace because he knows that he is loved."
Tranie Vo

That's my wife's contribution to the matter. Since that I will keep loving him for the rest of his life, how can I spare him the trauma of self-doubt and the process of healing. He is born with **Confidence**; all I have to do is not to break it!

That revelation changed the games of fatherhood to me. Instead of wishing the best of him and then to pressure him with expectations, I put the pressure on myself instead.

What kind of father should I become to be the role model that I wish my son will have?

Doing so, I was trained to be **SMART** and **STRONG**. That caused so much tension between my dad and I. I may be among the strongest and the smartest, but it was only painful, and maybe, all of that could have been avoided…

Until that point, I had no answer, just a hope, and an idea. I change the words of **SMART** and **STRONG** to **GENEROUS** and **FLEXIBLE**. Doing so, I had to train myself first to be both **GENEROUS** and **FLEXIBLE**.

It took some time, but I reached my goal. Today William is having all of them as a default model: **SMART** and **STRONG**, **GENEROUS**, and **FLEXIBLE**.

He is merely copying what he is exposed to. At 7, he wanted to write books because he saw me writing books. At 8, he pushed me to break my world record writing, just because he wanted more!

The first time I went up to give a speech in front of hundreds of people, I was in my thirties. William had his first at 8! As I was giving an address telling my story, he got interviewed on stage.

A few weeks later, he said that next time, he wanted to have his speech! I couldn't figure out what he meant by that. His explanation blew me out of the water: he wanted to be alone on stage and to tell his story, just like me! He's 8!

Never I would have thought that my son of 8 will be making the difference!

On the other hand, he shared with his mom how excited and nervous he was before going up on stage to speak. He is a kid with normal feelings. His feelings are mixed, but the strongest one is to be Dr. Bak!

In short, his feelings and ambition are simply the same: to be and, eventually, to beat Dr. Bak!

"He doesn't know the word CONFIDENCE
and what it means. He doesn't have to."
Dr. Bak Nguyen

What I learned looking at my son and evolving with him for now nearly nine years, is that:

Confidence is natural,

Confidence is love,

Confidence is free.

One can be broken and might spend one's life to reach back what one've lost. More then often, **Confidence** is shattered by those who cared for us. Why? Out of **INSECURITY** and **NEED TO CONTROL**.

As a dad, I learned to isolate my insecurities and kept them for myself. I bettered myself to give my son the most of what I am.

Doing so, I improved both my insurance and my **Confidence**. Doing so, I gave my son the alternative to never have to understand what it means to be **Confidence**; he needs to be, be.

That's the **POWER OF EMOTIONAL INTELLIGENCE**! No self-doubt, no insecurity, no expectation.

"Listen, accept, respect, and grow.
Those are the keys to Confidence."
Dr. Bak Nguyen

And **Confidence** is the key to **Influence**. Heal and let go. Accept and embrace the possibilities. We all have the potential to thrive, no to survive. We all have the right to be happy.

"We make our happiness!"
Dr. Bak Nguyen

Confidence is not only power; it is nature. Be in harmony with yours, and you will feel your power rising. You don't have to be the smartest, the strongest, or the wisest. You need to listen to yourself and to embrace who you are.

The **POWER OF EMOTIONAL INTELLIGENCE** is within each of us. It is waiting for every one of us to tap in and to bloom from its energy.

Welcome to **MILLION DOLLAR MINDSET**. This is **POWER, EMOTIONAL INTELLIGENCE**.

This book is not about understanding EMOTIONAL
INTELLIGENCE, but about accessing its POWER

Dr. BAK NGUYEN

CHAPTER 6
"TO FIND POWER"
by Dr. BAK NGUYEN

I can't believe that we are in chapter 6 already! It seems to me that we just started our journey yesterday... How do you feel so far?

Until now, we learned to gather intelligence thanks to **SYMPATHY** and **ACTIVE LISTENING**. Then, we learned to predict the future with **EMPATHY**. Then, we kicked it up a notch; we harnessed the power to draft the future with **INFLUENCE**.

Within three chapters, we gained awareness and much potential. As a double down, we added fuel and gas on the fire, building **MOMENTUM** with the **FORCE of the CROWD**, growing our **INFLUENCE** to the next level. Is this the ultimate level? We were only in chapter 4, what do you think?

It is great to see the vision, but to build that kind of power, one needs a strong base. Throughout this book, the key was:

"Align your emotions and your ambitions
to be whole, to be unstoppable."
Dr. Bak Nguyen

And to understand our emotions, we need to let them run free and then, to learn to tame and to evolve with them. Not to suppress or hide them away.

I am not talking about being a drama queen and to be an emotional bomb or a drag here. I am saying to be true to yourself and to accept your nature.

To see our ambitions, one needs to be strong enough to take a stand. Everybody wants something, but is it what you want or what someone else wants for you?

The only way to build from ambition is to stay right with ourselves. In other words, to be the one setting the expectations.

"Know yourself, know who you are dealing with, and then, you may deal."
Dr. Bak Nguyen

Easier said than done. How do you know someone before you have dealt with him/her? You will never know someone completely. They are changing, and so are you. All you can do is to learn to reassess and to adapt, constantly.

So if people are changing, some at a faster pace than others, but everybody is changing, it is possible to deal only with those you know... since you never really know everyone?

If you followed that line of thoughts, you would quickly conclude that to keep growing and to keep evolving; you will need to connect with more and new people. And how do you join, but by opening yourself up?

It will take courage to open up and to trust. Once again, the answer you seek starts from within. It is called **CONFIDENCE**.

"Confidence is to be whole and to in HARMONY."
Dr. Bak Nguyen

Each of us has to find their way to build their **Confidence**. Just like making money, there are thousands of ideas, and they are all hard to seek.

About **Confidence**, there are many ways, and they are demanding to walk, not just hard to seek.

"Confidence is a journey."
Dr. Bak Nguyen

A journey! It is sexy and appealing. It is free and must stay light to be useful.

Yes, Confidence must remain light to avoid to become pride. In most of my **QUEST OF IDENTITY**'s book, the **LEGENDARY** series, I describe PRIDE as a shield, a shield we often use to protect our weaknesses.

IDENTITY, THE ANTHOLOGY Of QUESTS (my 3rd book), **HYBRID** (my 11th book) and **FORCES OF NATURE** (my 15th book) all address the theme of **PRIDE**. I strongly recommend those reads for those of you looking for yourself.

On the matter of **Confidence**, I will state the following in this book:

"The fewer the words, the better."
Dr. Bak Nguyen

Just like writing a **QUOTE**, you want to keep your ideas focussed and straight to the point. The only way to do so is to dive in yourself completely, without holdback, without excuses, without fear.

If there is something you can be fearless about is undoubtedly to run in your yard! Even if this makes much sense, to run your yard is one of the most difficult journey one will face.

"One's story begins the day
one's quest of identity ends."
Dr. Bak Nguyen

To run your yard is to learn to know who you are. To learn to accept what you are, and to learn to respect what you've discovered. Only then, you might start your real journey, your destiny.

Facing such odds, it is often easier to practice on another field, one where we do not have as many burdens and handicaps from our emotions and denials. To learn from dealing with others!

On paper, this sounded harder, but it is much easier to start from the other and then bring it back to us. This might sound contra-intuitive, but because of **PRIDE**, because of **FEAR**, because of **DOUBT**, to deal with others will lead us to understand ourselves better.

To do so, we must find the courage to be open, to face the unknown and to learn from it. If you need a comparison, think of it this way:

"Even if the ocean is much closer to us,
it was easier to reach out in space
than to dive deep in the ocean."
Dr. Bak Nguyen

Think of the ocean as yourself and as space as the other. In the area, there is less pressure, less gravity, less attraction. Your weight is divided in space. That's how it feels like went you walk on the other's field.

In the deep of the ocean, the pressure is exponential, the weight is multiple, and gravity seems only to crush you. You might wet your feet on its edge; you don't know its true nature.

You might swim in for years, but unless you dive in deep, you are merely scratching the surface. That's pretty close to how it feels to fall in your pool of identity.

In the last chapter, I shared with you how I find and free my **Confidence**. I also shared with you how I nurture my son's **Confidence**. Two different stories, from different angles, but leading to the same outcome.

Through my story, you know how it feels. It was easier to dive in my ocean than to face our own. That's why I reversed the chapter, talking about me before I spoke of you.

You shared my pains and challenges. You also shared my hopes and joy. Now it is time for you to experiment yours. Not only from wetting your feet or from scratching the surface.

You were brave enough to go to space, to embrace the unknown going in other's people journey. You are ready to find your destiny and to face your demons because beyond the monsters; there is a world of wonders and powers.

The **Quest of Identity** is not one finding a name or a destiny. Part I is the quest to heal from your past and to find your whole. In other words, to be one with your emotions and one with your ambitions.

The **Quest of Identity** is the Quest for your **Confidence**. You will not find it in a hidden coffer at the bottom of the sea. You will find your **Confidence** diving in heavy water, facing your fears and your demons.

Then, as you understand that your demons are a part of you, you will stop fighting to embrace instead. That's the **HARMONY** and the whole that I am trying to push you forward to.

Once in **HARMONY**, your fears start to shrink, drastically. And as soon as your worries are shrinking, the pressure will lighten up, the light will touch the depth of your ocean, the water will feel warmer, and you are not swimming anymore, You are surfing and diving all at the same time.

That feeling of freedom is your graduation from your **Quest of Identity**.

The second part of the Quest of Identity is called your Destiny, your Legend. It is when you are looking for your purpose in Life and the materialization of your vision.

From both parts, nothing is secured, nothing is known. Everything will have to be discovered, tested and adapted. That's what makes it exciting.

Emotional Intelligence is not about what you know, but about what you feel. It is about what you've experienced. You've practiced and mastered the gathering of information from others. Now, do it on your yourself to find your **Confidence**.

You've mastered how to feel what the others think from **EMPATHY**. Have a taste of your own medicine by allowing you to contact your own emotions, the ones you hid in the depth of your soul, your ocean. That will enable you to find your **HARMONY**, and by extension, your **powers**.

"To be in HARMONY is to be

at peace with oneself."
Dr. Bak Nguyen

Find the courage to dive, face your demons, and make t your allies. Embrace your whole and find your happiness.

Welcome to **MILLION DOLLAR MINDSET**. This is **POWER, EMOTIONAL INTELLIGENCE**.

This book is not about understanding EMOTIONAL INTELLIGENCE but about accessing its POWER
Dr. BAK NGUYEN

CHAPTER 7
"TO BE POWER"
by Dr. BAK NGUYEN

It is exhilarating. Can you believe that you had all that power inside of you? Confidence is the key to power. With that key, you've just unlocked the toolbox of **EMOTIONAL INTELLIGENCE**.

EMOTIONAL INTELLIGENCE is many things. It covers from body language reading to Leverage and Confidence. I am so proud of you; together, we went far beyond the scope of what was intended.

Went I first started this book, **POWER, EMOTIONAL INTELLIGENCE**, I was planning to cover body language and psychology. Since, I went with what I knew best, emotions, and evolution.

I will leave the other angle of body language and psychology to the experts of those fields.

Yes, we are about to finish this journey together. We've covered much ground from intelligence gathering to **Confidence** and the power of the crowd.

After the knowledge of building **Momentums** from the **Influence** to move a crowd, what is next? Is there something even bigger? Yes, there is. It was big enough for me to choose it over covering body language!

"I am lazy. What was supposed to be a liability turned out to be a blessing, one I learned to leverage on."
Dr. Bak Nguyen

This is not the first time, nor the last time that you will hear me saying that I am lazy. By lazy, I meant that I don't like to work. I want to play. I like to win.

By lazy, I meant that I will always find and use all the shortcuts available to reach a goal. The fastest, the better, is speed is my essence. See? I am learning to respect myself!

I won't cheat, but I will play the games where I can bend the rules and raise the average, just like writing books. I started of fear of speaking in public, the fear of speaking after the former first lady, Michelle Obama (the complete story in the **POWER OF YES**).

Then, I learned and mastered the next craft and skill. I started to enjoy sharing and writing. It took me a few months, but then, I decided to go all in! How about breaking world records writing books?

I am not writing to break world records; I am breaking world records because I am writing! That's not the same thing, at not at all!

My victories today are side effects of my being and state of mind; they are not goals anymore. That's how I gained in power and inefficiency, writing from 15 books within 15 months to 8 children's book in a month, the following month. From there, I went from 36 papers within 18 months + 1 week.

For those of you who are following my story, I have hard facts proving that recognition is now a side effect of my journey. How I came to write with William, my kid, was because I wanted to keep my promise to an eight years old child.

I've included the writing of the French versions because he was failing his French classes.

We've pushed up to 8 books because he didn't want to stop and I loved the idea of infinite. All of those were the motivations, the recognitions are still pending, and that does not change what we are or what we do.

If anything, it fuelled my passion for sharing even more and at an even higher pace! I recently finished my 20th months as a writer with 40 books written. For the 21st months, so far, I will have completed 43 books, including this one!

Yes, I am riding my **Momentum** thanks to my **Confidence** and the people around me. Would you like to know the next phase to **Emotional Intelligence**?

Attraction. The attraction is the next key to Emotional Intelligence. Draw because it makes everything easier. Instead of going to people, people are coming to you with the **POWER OF ATTRACTION**.

Instead of grinding to build up an audience, your fans are running after you and eating up each of your words. **ATTRACTION**, that's **Momentum** for the lazy people!

To gain and master **ATTRACTION** is an art and a state of mind. First of all, you must be calm, really calm. Even if you are passionate, you cannot look excited.

Don't get me wrong, there is nothing wrong about being excited, but the message that you are sending is that it is a phase that might pass since it requires much energy to maintain. When you appear calm, people are associating that with a natural state.

Since most people are scared of change, being calm will put them at ease.

> *"The easiest way to implement change*
> *is without resistance."*
> Dr. Bak Nguyen

That by itself is almost impossible. But it is a goal to aim toward. So stay calm to attract people.

Just like writing, you will need to be **bold** and **honest**. By being **bold**, you are branding yourself with a core message; one people can follow and be inspired from. By being **honest**,... do I really have to say it?

But just in case, by being **honest**, that's your first means of communication. If you have people trust, you can dialogue with them. Otherwise, you are just a salesperson!

But let's go back at being **bold** for a minute. Being **bold** doesn't mean to be arrogant. Being **bold** means to have enough courage to lay out your ideas, and you announce your path of action.

You are **bold** means to have taken the time to reflect on the matter, to have weighed the pros and cons and to have the courage to make a clear decision about your choices and the course of action.

When you shared not just the conclusions, but the whole process with your audience, you are sharing with them two things: one, your thought process allowing them to visualize their journey with you and two; you are giving them direction.

The truth is that most of them will only hear the direction, and as they feel good about it, they will be following the crowd. You now have to make sure that the group is behind you!

To be **calm** is the first key to **Attraction**. The second key is to be **bold**. Those two, we covered already. The third key is to be **kind**. To be **kind** in all its forms.

When you are **kind**, you are caring to want what is best for those you are sharing with. When you are **kind**, you do not seek control, nor influences, you are seeking results, their results.

Some times, you might want what is right for them more than they want it themselves. This is where the tension starts to rise. How to care and when to stop is a diffuse and challenging line. Trust me on that; I've burned myself more than once, trying to do good.

The key is **Respect**. In medicine, you cannot treat a patient unless he/she agrees to the treatment. Even if you have taken an oath to not harm, you cannot heal someone who is refusing help. That's the law, that's also a **law of nature**.

"Don't try to help someone who doesn't want help.
He will be fighting you through each step of the way,
and you will be the villain of the story."
Dr. Bak Nguyen

There is no justice here, just plain stupidity. Be kind, be generous, but don't force others. On that, my **Influence** on my son led us to write the following:

"I will show you. I will not force you.
But I won't wait for you."
William Bak & Dr. Bak Nguyen

So be kind, really kind. Be kind enough to care. Be kind enough to respect. Be kind enough to tolerate.

The world is not yours to command, only yours to serve if the people choose so.

And people are not duped, they can feel who cares and who don't. If my proteges are attracted to me because of my leadership, I draw the attention of great mentors because I am sensitive and that they can feel the caring side.

Don't get me wrong, mentors, especially the **"five stars generals"** they don't expect you to be smart and robust, they assume that you are. Those are prerequisites. Even so, the world is full of intelligent and healthy people; what they are looking for is also leaders with their heart in the right place.

In most of my friendship with my mentors, to have fun was the key ingredient to our relationship. And of course, at this level, we are having fun building and scoring something.

> "Words are strong and bold;
> actions must follow and beat the words."
> Dr. Bak Nguyen

This is how I managed to attract more powerful and more magnificent mentors and friends around me. I often ask myself what those great people see in me.

Every time that I dare raised the question, the answer is always the same, my vibe and where my heart is: I care. Some will say that I am a gambler, some will say that I am creative, other will say that I speak too much, but all will say that they feel that I care and that I am merely warming up!

The **Power of Attraction** allowed me to make new friends and allies. Some of them became mentors and best friends. Those friendships boost my

Confidence and my experiences as I learned from the words and the stories.

It wasn't hard work or contacts that brought me where I am today. I was my **Emotional Intelligence** and its trails, my actions. People are reacting to what I am, and people are acting accordingly.

Once again, be and don't expect. Be **Confident** and share without expectation. Be **Kind** and help without imposing yourself. How people react is not of your concern; it is theirs.

Mind your own business and keep being **kind**, **generous**, flexible, **open**, and **confident**.

You have much to offer and so much more to share. Find your **Confidence** and fuel on your powers, those of **Momentum**, of **Attraction**, of **Influence**, of **Empathy**.

You now possess the three keys to the next phase of **Emotional Intelligence**, the keys to the **Power of Attraction**: **Calm**, **Bold**, and **Kind**.

You have the Power, you are the Power, thank your **Emotional Intelligence**.

Welcome to **MILLION DOLLAR MINDSET**. This is **POWER, EMOTIONAL INTELLIGENCE**.

This book is not about understanding EMOTIONAL INTELLIGENCE, but about accessing its POWER

Dr. BAK NGUYEN

CHAPTER 8

"TO SERVE THE GREATER"

by Dr. BAK NGUYEN

I sincerely don't know what else I can bring to you at this stage of your awareness of **Emotional Intelligence**. I gave you what I know and what I am doing on the matter.

Maybe one last thing…

Believe

Why is it of interest and importance in here? To **Believe** and **Confidence** goes hand in hand. The easiest to achieve is to **Believe** first. Then, **Confidence** will follow.

The best example of this concept is **Religion**. Many people believe in God and what they are told from Religion, but they lack complete confidence in themselves.

It is not wrong, just that you can't relate to God and others to do the job for you.

"I believe in myself, and I do it for God,
not the other way around."
Dr. Bak Nguyen

Not to offend anyone here, but this is how we can move forward, how anyone can move forward. To bet on ourselves and to do it for God. This is my recipe, and it served me well until now.

On the same line of thoughts, to know the other first and then, to learn to know about ourselves is more comfortable. You can believe in something else early to discover the **howto**.

Then, you can apply the process of thinking to yourself. Once again, it might be contra-intuitive, but it works like a charm.

I talked about Religion. I grew up with religion, and I never had the choice, it was chosen for me long before I knew there was even a question.

At some point in my life, I knew much of the stories in the bible by heart. Then I started raising questions, questions that people didn't like.

I had my faith whole when I was raising what I thought was a simple question. I didn't even evaluate their answers, the simple fact that it put them in such disarray and emotional distress told me a big part of their story: their Faith and understanding were pretty weak!

The more they were doubting, the more they were mad at my questions. It was not about God; it was about them! Without their Faith in Religion, they were emptied, filled with doubts and insecurities.

That era of my life taught me much about my surroundings and mindset. The Truth started to show through the painting…

Because I was raised to believe, I guess, that was my blueprint for evolving, believing in myself. That capability to think saved me from simply drowning while I needed to grow my **Confidence** and to heal.

I used the same template of belief, but I was looking to believe in myself. I kept honoring God as a superior being to whom I was held accountable.

The fears I had, I managed to transpose them in the next Life, at the **final judgment**, as I will be facing my creator. I told you that I knew much about the bible. I based much of my life on the story of the **Master and his three servants**.

The Master had to go away for a year and called his three servants. He gave three talents to the first one, two to the second and one to the last one. In roman's time, ability is money... I guess, today we use it to play with the words...

A year later, the Master returns and asks to see his servants. The first one presented himself and gave back the three talents that he received in addition to three more. The second gave back two and two.

The last one knew that he wasn't as talented and was scared to lose what he received. He dug a hole in the ground and hid it.

As the Master was back, he went out and dug out his talent and ran to his Master, showing one dirty ability, rotten and single!

The Master was furious and fired the servant saying that he was a lazy, worthless piece of … Then, he took a single talent and gave it to the one with six.

The moral of the story is that you have to make the most of what you've received. That, I learned from the bible.

"Justice is not to give to those who have none,
but to give to those worthy."
Dr. Bak Nguyen

Once, I had a dream. I was standing in front of God, and I was showing him my talents. I was pretty confident, almost cocky and sure of myself: "God, you gave me three talents, here there are, and here are three more."

Then God stood up, surprised! He looked down on me asking: "Three?! I gave you ten!?!" I woke up all sweaty. That spoiled the mood and the vibe of the rest of the night and the following day.

Never I want to face that situation, showing less than what is expected of me, out of time to fix my mistake.

From that day forward, the only real fear I have is to face God, unworthy. Doing so, I've transposed most of my concern to the next life… and I am free to act in this one!

You wanted an example of leveraging **Emotional Intelligence**; this is a great one! I used my **Emotional Intelligence** to managed to have a life fearless!

"To move forward, make leverage out
of your liability."
Dr. Bak Nguyen

Believe, is the first step to chance. As you believe, Hope will follow. From **Belief** and, **Hope, Confidence** will eventually follow as you bet on yourself to make things happen.

Some words are more potent than others. Those three will make the difference between survival life of challenges and a thriving adventure related as legends.

Because yes, you can be a side character in someone else story or the hero of your legend. You do not need to be anything more than what you are nor anyone else to shine; you need to find yourself.

Emotional Intelligence is free; it was there all along. It is called **Instincts**, **Intuition**, **Emotions**, and **Confidence**. It goes way beyond your mind; it is higher than your heart; it is your whole!

"Our tendency to cut everything into smaller parts to accommodate our understanding made us lose sight of the big picture and the whole."
Dr. Bak Nguyen

Stop trying to understand and to impose your limited logic. Free yourself to feel, and you will understand what's natural.

So I guess, the best part of being **Emotionally Intelligent** is that you do not have to be smart... you have to accept and to respect your true nature.

Unlike most of the rest of life, by being **Emotionally Intelligent**, you do not take anything away from anyone. For once, it is not about a race anymore. It is about the awareness you have of yourself and your surroundings.

"Greater than a skill or a craft, are the respect and awareness of oneself."
Dr. Bak Nguyen

Feel to understand, live to feel. There is no other way to know what we are truly made of. Soon or later, we will have to face the mirror and, eventually, God.

Each time, if we know what we've received, we have the chance to present what we've become, multiple. Or, if fear got the best of us, we will give a single, a rotten one. But still, we will have to present.

It is neither hard or easy; it is a force of habit and a game of **Momentum**:

"The more one does, the more one will succeed, every day, day after day."
Dr. Bak Nguyen

It does not have to be hard. Find your fun, and it will feel like a game. Know what is your joy, your preferences, your loves, and stir Life accordingly.

That's the logic of **Emotional Intelligence**, to stir Life, so we feel empowered and at our best. And to shake Life, one must believe he has it in him to know what to do with freedom, with choice, with power.

"Only be being kind and by believing that one can hope of a better future."
Dr. Bak Nguyen

Believe, believe in life, believe in us, believe in you. If you believe, you are opening the door to something that is not, but maybe, will be. It is called **Hope**.

With **Hope**, if you keep believing, eventually, it will become a certitude, even if it is not, yet. As soon as you are convinced and sure, you have to find the strength and the courage to believe in yourself. This is called **Confidence**.

From **Confidence**, you now have the **Power to Influence** and to ride the future, all of it possible thank to your **Emotional Intelligence**.

Welcome to **MILLION DOLLAR MINDSET**. This is **POWER, EMOTIONAL INTELLIGENCE**.

The book is not about understanding EMOTIONAL INTELLIGENCE, but about accessing its POWER

Dr. BAK NGUYEN

CONCLUSION

"THE BLUEPRINT"

by Dr. BAK NGUYEN

This is not the end of your journey in **EMOTIONAL INTELLIGENCE**, merely the beginning. I have shared with you not theories or but the roots of the **WHY**, **WHAT**, **WHEN**, **WHERE**, and **HOW** of my understanding of **EMOTIONAL INTELLIGENCE**.

It is a unique take on the subject with the hope to empower you to find your our powers and your destiny.

From **SYMPATHY**, having others opening up to you, to **ACTIVE LISTENING**, saving you time and energy, from

EMPATHY, allowing you to predict the future to **INFLUENCE**, enabling you to draft the future, not to forget the power of the crowd with **MOMENTUM**, you are now in possession of power in tune with nature, yourself.

That was the first half of **POWER, EMOTIONAL INTELLIGENCE**. Then we went backward to cover the prerequisites. How to build a strong **CONFIDENCE**, how to be in **HARMONY**, how to leverage on **ATTRACTION**, and how to **BELIEVE**.

Logic will usually start from the beginning, starting from **BELIEVING** to end up with **MOMENTUM** in a crescendo. But doing so, will we have a slow, very slow beginning learning the basis patiently without a clear goal until the 2/3 of the book.

I don't like to play with your faith or patience. I dropped logic to embrace **EMOTIONAL INTELLIGENCE** instead, starting with what you can do with new power. I showed you the conventional wisdom and its flaws. Then, as I had your interest, I gave you an alternative.

From that point, I gained your trust, or at least, your interest. That was the first chapter. Then, we built up our journey surfing on the wave from Gathering information efficiently to predict the future. Once again, you were hooked!

At chapter 2, you felt like we knew each other for years by then. That's to show you how strong our bond was developing. All because I gave you up front the hidden secrets that you wish you might find somewhere by the end of your journey.

I didn't stop there; I was having fun too! I doubled down on your expectations, giving you now a way to **write the future** with **INFLUENCE**.

In the introduction, I talked about body language and different skills… we were so beyond the reading skill at this stage. We were still in chapter 3!

I know, some of you are overwhelmed with the new powers, that was the intention. You can learn and understand a piece of knowledge. A power, you have to feel it to be one with it. There is no other way.

Just like in a concert, I teased you a little more only to come back with an even higher power, raising the energy: **MOMENTUM**, to harness the **power of the crowd**!

You felt great; you felt empowered. I got you "graduated" at half of this book. And then, I did wish you luck on your journey. By that point, you were reading my lips to wonder what was coming next.

You were holding the book in your hand and yet, your body wandered if it was over, or what more could I bring to you. I went diving back to the source. The wording and the pace changed drastically. It was time to cool it down and to let the dust settle.

We became closer, sharing confidences. Now that I got your full attention, that I showed you the possibilities, it was easier for you to get back at the beginning and to realize what you missed and how to course correct.

CONFIDENCE, **RESPECT**, **HARMONY**, those are all words you knew. Now you have a reason to revisit your understanding and your beliefs. Usually, you'll be doing that with resistance, but since you had a taste of the power, the strength is gone, by magic, thanks to your **EMOTIONS**.

"Emotions can raise walls or calm the storm.
It's up to you to stir them."
Dr. Bak Nguyen

Because you were invested and interested, the beginning wasn't as dull and slow anymore. I then teased you a little more giving you the power of **ATTRACTION**. That was to remind you of the hype we shared three chapters earlier.

And then, I sat down next to you, talking about Belief, opening up myself to you and giving you the key to start.

Usually, what do we remember the most? You are right, the last thing. I gave you the last word as what you need to do to start your journey.

Laying out like this, it all makes sense. But from logic, I went all backward... Do you see my point? Even my conclusion is different; I wanted to continue with our proximity. I raised the curtain and showed you the blueprint of **EMOTIONAL INTELLIGENCE** I got you to experience.

It's all about feeling and experimenting. That's all. Now you know, and you are ready to be… powerful.

You have fresh in your mind how to start, by believing. After putting that to the test, you will have forgotten what is next… it doesn't matter! For as long as you've started, the rest will fall in place naturally.

After believing in yourself, **Confidence** will raise consequently. With **Confidence**, **Attraction** will follow. As you have people surrounding you, you will then make a mistake to listen without a blueprint… and then, you will remember something about:

"Everyone lies."
Dr. Gregory House

A smile will stick to your face for the rest of that day. Then, you will come back and read the first chapters of this book to master your skills and your emotions.

We all have to start from the beginning, but I've spent too much time at school to know that it is not how we enjoyed learning. We need a strong motivation, and as we stumbled on the field, to get back up on our feet was fuelled with our desire to crack the secret.

That's believing! That's conviction! That's something we can build on.

The whole purpose of **POWER, EMOTIONAL INTELLIGENCE** was to get you to start. Soon enough, you won't be able to stop; you won't want to stop.

That's how we build **MOMENTUM** by getting you started. Now go! Go to start your journey and find your powers. I won't be too far.

We will meet again. My brothers and sisters in arms, I salute you.

Welcome to **MILLION DOLLAR MINDSET**. This is **POWER, EMOTIONAL INTELLIGENCE**.

This book is not about understanding EMOTIONAL INTELLIGENCE, but about accessing its POWER
Dr. BAK NGUYEN

FROM THE SAME AUTHOR
Dr. Bak Nguyen

TITLES AVAILABLE AT

www.DrBakNguyen.com

MAJOR LEAGUES' ACCESS

FACTEUR HUMAIN
LE LEADERSHIP DU SUCCÈS
par DR BAK NGUYEN & CHRISTIAN TRUDEAU

ehappyPedia
THE RISE OF THE UNICORN
BY DR. BAK NGUYEN & DR. JEAN DE SERRES

CHAMPION MINDSET
LEARNING TO WIN
BY DR. BAK NGUYEN & CHRISTOPHE MULUMBA

BRANDING DR.BAK
BALANCING STRATEGY AND EMOTIONS
BY DR. BAK NGUYEN, BRENDA GARCIA & SANTIAGO CHICA

BUSINESS

La Symphonie des Sens
ENTREPREUNARIAT
par DR BAK NGUYEN

Industries Disruptors
BY DR. BAK NGUYEN, ROUBA SAKR AND COLLABORATORS

Changing the World from a dental chair
BY DR. BAK NGUYEN

The Power Behind the Alpha
BY TRANIE VO & DR. BAK NGUYEN

SELFMADE
GRATITUDE AND HUMILITY
BY DR. BAK NGUYEN

CHILDREN'S BOOK
with William Bak

The Trilogy of Legends

THE LEGEND OF THE CHICKEN HEART
BY DR. BAK NGUYEN & WILLIAM BAK

THE LEGEND OF THE LION HEART
BY DR. BAK NGUYEN & WILLIAM BAK

THE LEGEND OF THE DRAGON HEART
BY DR. BAK NGUYEN & WILLIAM BAK

WE ARE ALL DRAGONS
BY DR. BAK NGUYEN & WILLIAM BAK

THE 9 SECRETS OF THE **SMART CHICKEN**
BY DR. BAK NGUYEN & WILLIAM BAK

THE SECRET OF THE **FAST CHICKEN**
BY DR. BAK NGUYEN & WILLIAM BAK

THE LEGEND OF THE **SUPER CHICKEN**
BY DR. BAK NGUYEN & WILLIAM BAK

THE STORY OF THE **CHICKEN SHIT**
BY DR. BAK NGUYEN & WILLIAM BAK

WHY **CHICKEN** CAN'T DREAM?
BY DR. BAK NGUYEN & WILLIAM BAK

LEGENDARY

IDENTITY
THE ANTHOLOGY OF QUESTS
BY DR. BAK NGUYEN

HYBRID
THE MODERN QUEST OF IDENTITY
BY DR. BAK NGUYEN

FORCES OF NATURE
FORGING THE CHARACTER OF WINNERS
BY DR. BAK NGUYEN

LIFESTYLE

HORIZON, BUILDING UP THE VISION
VOLUME ONE
BY DR. BAK NGUYEN

MILLION DOLLAR MINDSET

MOMENTUM TRANSFER
BY DR. BAK NGUYEN & Coach DINO MASSON

LEVERAGE
COMMUNICATION INTO SUCCESS
BY DR. BAK NGUYEN AND COLLABORATORS

THE POWER OF YES
MY 18 MONTHS JOURNEY
BY DR. BAK NGUYEN

HOW TO WRITE A BOOK IN 30 DAYS
BY DR. BAK NGUYEN

POWER
EMOTIONAL INTELLIGENCE
BY DR. BAK NGUYEN

MENTORS
BY DR. BAK NGUYEN

HOW TO NOT FAIL AS A DENTIST
BY DR. BAK NGUYEN

PARENTING

THE BOOK OF LEGENDS
BY DR. BAK NGUYEN & WILLIAM BAK

THE BOOK OF LEGENDS 2
BY DR. BAK NGUYEN & WILLIAM BAK

PERSONAL GROWTH

REBOOT
MIDLIFE CRISIS
BY DR. BAK NGUYEN

PHILOSOPHY

LEADERSHIP
PANDORA'S BOX
BY DR. BAK NGUYEN

KRYPTO
TO SAVE THE WORLD
BY DR. BAK NGUYEN & ILYAS BAKOUCH

PROFESSION HEALTH
THE UNCONVENTIONAL QUEST OF HAPPINESS
BY DR. BAK NGUYEN, DR. MIRJANA SINDOLIC,
DR. ROBERT DURAND AND COLLABORATORS

WHITE COATS
THE UNCONVENTIONAL QUEST OF HAPPINESS
BY DR. BAK NGUYEN AND COLLABORATORS

LE RÊVE CANADIEN
D'IMMIGRANT À MILLIONNAIRE
par DR BAK NGUYEN

TITLES AVAILABLE AT

www.DrBakNguyen.com

DR.

Bak Nguyen

www.DrBakNguyen.com